ASP.NET MVC 5

Your First Guide-

From Zero Steps to Confident User

By Jordan Rees

Table of Contents

Disclaimer

While all attempts have been made to verify the information provided in this book, the author does assume any responsibility for errors, omissions, or contrary interpretations of the subject matter contained within. The information provided in this book is for educational and entertainment purposes only. The reader is responsible for his or her own actions and the author does not accept any responsibilities for any liabilities or damages, real or perceived, resulting from the use of this information.

The trademarks that are used are without any consent, and the publication of the trademark is without permission or backing by the trademark owner. All trademarks and brands within this book are for clarifying purposes only and are the owned by the owners themselves, not affiliated with this document.

Introduction

The objective of most programmers especially the web developers is to create applications which are easy to test, deploy, maintain and debug in case errors occur. However, this is a challenge to most of them. ASP.NET introduced the use of MVC (model, view and controller) framework which can assist them in this. ASP.NET MVC 5 makes use of this in the way that the application is divided into the above three layers.

It is possible for the three layers to communicate with each other. Applications developed by making use of this framework are always easy to change in case there is a need for this in the future. It is highly encouraged that developers should make use of this framework for developing their web apps and other apps.

Chapter 1- Definition

ASP.NET is a web framework and it employs the use of the Model-View-Controller pattern. It is an open-source framework. Software developed using this have three roles, the model, the view and the controller. Web applications developed using this framework have three layers which include the following:

- Model- which is the business layer.
- View- which is the display layer.
- Controller- acts as the input controller.

The model is used to represent the state in which a particular aspect of an application is. The controller is responsible for handling the interactions between the model and the view. It keeps the model up-to-date by propagating the changes made in either the view or the controller to the model.

It is also responsible for passing of information between the two layers. The view has the task of accepting information from the controller. It then displays this information on the user interface for viewing by the users. The framework works on the server side of the application and is responsible for producing dynamic web pages for the application.

Microsoft was responsible for development of ASP.Net MVC 5 and their aim was to help developers in developing dynamic websites, web application and web pages. In this framework, each of the components, that is, the model, the view, and the controller can be tested independently from each other component.

Chapter 2- Getting Started

For you to start programming in ASP.NET MVC 5, you need to begin by installing either *"visual studio"* or *"visual studio express for web"*. Any version of these can work. They are also available online for free download. Visual studio is a Microsoft product and it is the IDE (Integrated Development Environment) used for development in ASP.NET. After launching this IDE, you will see a bar at the top which shows numerous options which are available to you.

A menu which gives you other options on how to carry out tasks in visual studio is also available. A good example is when creating a new project. You can just open the IDE and click on *"File -> New -> Project"* rather than clicking on *"New Project"* on the start page.

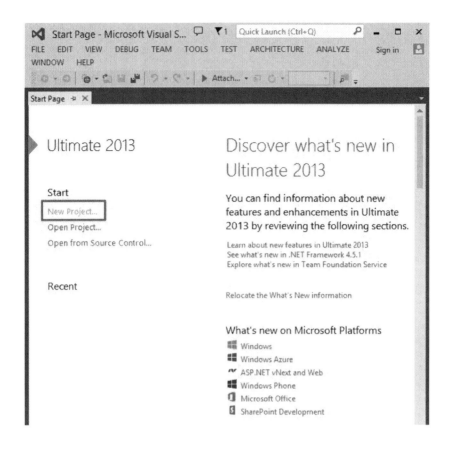

How to create an Application

We want to create our new and first application in visual studio.

Follow the procedure below:

1. Click on "*New Project*".

2. On the left, choose *"visual c#"*. Select *"Web"* and then choose *"ASP.NET Web Application"*.

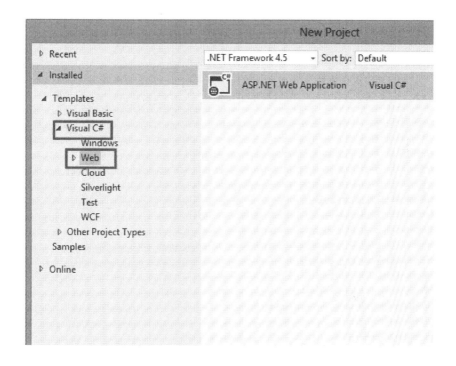

3. Provide a name of choice to your application and then click on the *"ok"* button.

4. A dialog will appear. Click on *"MVC"* and then click on the *"ok"* button.

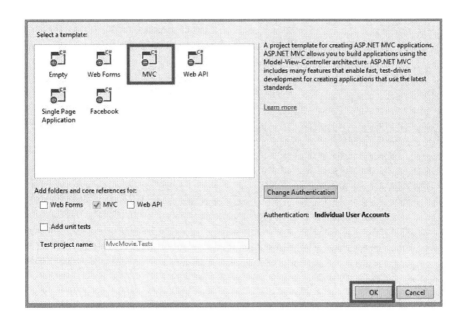

Your application will then be ready to be run. Any application newly created in ASP.Net comes with a default *"Hello World!"* application. After the above procedure, you will be presented with the following interface:

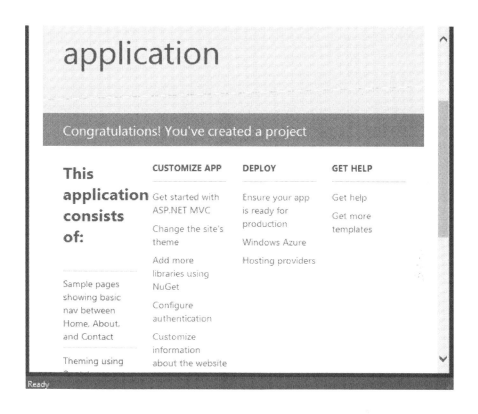

If you need to start debugging your application, you have to press the "*F5*" key on your keyboard. IIS Express will be started and this will cause your application to run. Your browser will be opened and the home page of your application will be displayed.

If you look at the address or the URL of the application, you will notice that it has the word "*localhost*" and a port number. The word "*localhost*" points to your own computer, and this is where your application is hosted and being run. The port number is picked randomly by your application, so don't be panicked when you see it change once you run the application a second time.

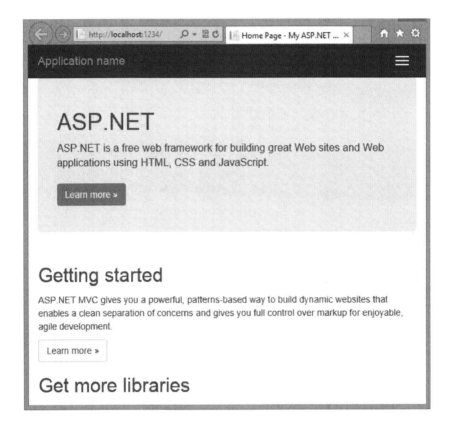

The page will have the "*Home*", "*Contact*" and "*About*" pages. You might not be able to see them at the moment, which might be due to the size of the browser. You might have to use the navigation bar to be able to see these. You might have to click on the *"Menu"* icon to see these links.

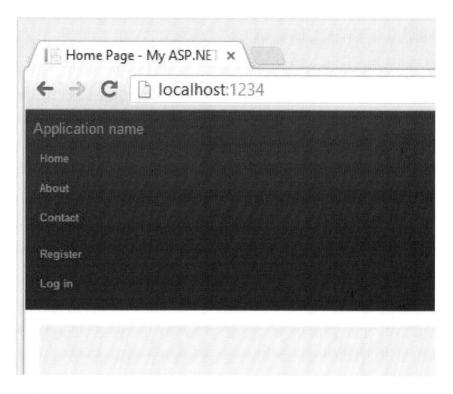

With the application, it is also possible to register and then login. These are shown in the above figure. Note that this is the default application, so you have done nothing to it. You need to change how it works so as to get what you want. This calls for learning to program in ASP.NET MVC. You need to change its code so as to achieve your goal.

Chapter 3- Routing in MVC

In Web Forms Application for Asp.Net, each URL has to be matched to a specific .aspx file. A good example is the URL http://domain/employeesinfo.aspx, which has to be matched to the file named employeesinfo.aspx. This file should have the code and the markup, which can be rendered on a browser.

The routing process was introduced in ASP.Net as a way of eliminating the process of mapping each URL to a specific file. With routing, we are able to specify the URL pattern that will be matched to a request handler. The request handler in this case can be a class or a file.

For the case of a webform application, the request handler has to be an .aspx file, while in MVC; it has to be the Controller class and an Action method.

The URL http://domain/employees may be mapped to http://domain/employeesinfo.aspx **in the ASP.NET** Webforms, while in MVC; this URL has to be mapped to the Student Controller and the Index action.

All the configured routes for an application are kept in a routing table and the Routing engine uses them to determine the appropriate handler file or class for the incoming request.

Each MVC application has to configure at least a single route that is configured by the MVC framework by default. The configuration of a route has to be done in the RouteConfig class, which can be found in RouteConfig.cs under the App_Start folder.

The URL pattern is only considered after the part for the domain part in a URL. A good example is the URL "{controller}/{action}/{id}", which would appear as "localhost:1234/{controller}/{action}/{id}".

Anything that appears after the "localhost:1234/" will be referred to as the controller name. Anything which appears after the controller name will be an action name followed by the value of the id parameter.

For a URL that has nothing after the domain name, the default controller and the action method will be used for handling the request. A good example is the **http://lcoalhost:1234,** which will be handled by the HomeController and the Index method as it has been configured in the defaults parameter. Below we have a list of Controllers, action methods and Ids for handling the different URLS:

1. http://localhost/home- this will be handled by the HomeController, Index Action method, and null Id.

2. http://localhost/home/index/123- this will be handled by the HomeController, Index Action method, and 123 Id.

3. http://localhost/home/about- this will be handled by the HomeController, About Action method, and null Id.

4. http://localhost/home/contact- this will be handled by the HomeController, Contact Action method, and null Id.

5. http://localhost/student- this will be handled by the StudentController, Index Action method, and null Id.

6. http://localhost/student/edit/123- this will be handled by the StudentController, Edit Action method, and 123 Id.

Multiple Routes

A custom route can also be configured using a MapRoute extension method. At least two parameters should be provided in the MapRoute: a route name and the URL pattern.

Consider the example given below, which shows how an Employee route can be configured:

```
public class RouteConfig
{
    public static void RegisterRoutes(RouteCollection routes)
    {

        routes.IgnoreRoute("{resource}.axd/{*pathInfo}");

        routes.MapRoute(
            name: "Employee",
            url: "employees/{id}",
            defaults: new { controller = "Employee", action = "Index"}
        );

        routes.MapRoute(
            name: "Default",
            url: "{controller}/{action}/{id}",
```

```
        defaults: new { controller = "Home", action =
"Index", id = UrlParameter.Optional }

    );

  }

}
```

As shown above, the Employee route has the URL pattern of *employees/{id}*, which is a specification that any URL that begins with domainName/employees has to be handled by the EmployeesController.

Note that no {action} was specified in the URL pattern, since our aim is that each URL that begins with employee should use an EmployeesController Index action. The default controller has been specified together with the action for handling any URL request that starts from the domainname/employees.

Route Constraints

Restrictions can be applied to the value of the parameter through configuration of the route constraints. Consider the route given below, which applies a restriction to the id parameter that specifies that the values of the id have to be numeric:

routes.MapRoute(

    name: "Employee",

    url: "employee/{id}/{name}/{standardId}",

    defaults: new { controller = "Employee", action = "Index", id = UrlParameter.Optional, name = UrlParameter.Optional, standardId = UrlParameter.Optional },

    constraints: new { id = @"\d+" }

  );

This means that if you are given a non-numeric value for the id parameter, the request will be handled by another route, and if matching routes are not found, then you will get a "The resource could not be found" error.

Register Routes

Once all routes have been configured in the RouteConfig class, then you have to register it in the Application_Start() event in Global.asax. This will mean that it will have all the routes in a routing table:

```
public class MvcApplication :
System.Web.HttpApplication
    {
        protected void Application_Start()
        {

RouteConfig.RegisterRoutes(RouteTable.Routes);
        }
    }
```

This shows how important routing is in an MVC framework. It maps a URL to a physical file or class, or to the controller class in the MVC. The route has URL pattern as well as handler information. The URL pattern begins after the domain name.

The routes may be configured in the RouteConfig class and you can also configure multiple custom routes. The route constraints are used for applying restrictions on parameter values. The route should also be configured in the event Application_Start in the Global.ascx.cs file.

Chapter 4- Action Method, Action Selectors and Action Verbs

The controller class usually has the action method, which will be discussed in this section. All the public methods that are contained in a Controller class are known as Action methods. These are just like the normal methods but they have the restrictions given below:

1. All action methods should be public. It can't be a protected or a private method.
2. You cannot overload action methods.
3. Action methods cannot be static methods.

An Index method is a public method that returns ActionResult using the view() method. The definition of the view() method is done in the Controller base class, and it returns the necessary ActionResult.

Default Action method

Each controller may have a default action method based on the configured route in the RouteConfig class. The default setting is that the Index is a default action method for a controller, as demonstrated below:

```
routes.MapRoute(
    name: "Default",
    url: "{controller}/{action}/{id}/{name}",
    defaults: new { controller = "Home",
            action = "Index",
            id = UrlParameter.Optional
    });
```

However, it is possible to change the default action name depending on what you need in the RouteConfig class.

ActionResult

There are various result classes in the MVC framework, which can be returned from the action methods. These result classes usually represent the different types of responses such as html, string, file, javascript, json, and others.

ActionResult class forms the base class for all result classes, meaning that it can form the return of any of the action methods returning any results. However, you can specify the necessary result class as the return type of the action method.

The Index() method for EmployeeController class uses the View() method to return the ViewResult. This is usually derived from the ActionResult. The definition of the View() method is done in the base controller class. This also has different methods, and they return a particular type of result.

Action method Parameters

Each action method may have input parameters as the normal methods. These can be either complete data type or primitive data type parameters. The following example best demonstrates this:

[HttpPost]

public ActionResult Edit(Employee dept)

{

    // update employee to the database

    return RedirectToAction("Index");

}

[HttpDelete]

public ActionResult Delete(int id)

{

    // delete employee from the database where the id matches with the //specified id

```
    return RedirectToAction("Index");
}
```

The default setting is that the values for the action method are obtained from the data collection of the request. The data collection features name/value pairs for the form data, the query strings values, or the cookie values.

Action Selectors

This refers to an attribute that is applicable to action methods. It works to help the routine engine choose the correct action method for handling a particular request. The following are the available action selectors in MVC 5:

1. ActionName

2. NonAction

3. ActionVerbs

This one is responsible for allowing us to specify a different action name rather than the method name. Consider the example given below:

```
public class EmployeeController : Controller
{

    public EmployeeController()
    {

    }
    [ActionName("find")]
    public ActionResult GetById(int id)
    {
        // get employee from the database
        return View();
    }
}
```

In the example given above, we have applied the attribute named "ActionName("find")" to the GetById action method. This means that our action name will be "find" rather than "GetById". The action method will then be invoked in the http://localhost/employee /find/1 request rather than on the request http://localhost/employee/getbyid/1.

NonAction

The NonAction selector attribute usually specifies that the public action method for a controller isn't an action method. You should use this attribute when you need a public method but you don't need to treat this as an action method. The public method named GetEmployee() cannot be invoked in a similar manner as the action method as shown in the example given below:

public class EmployeeController : Controller

{

```
public EmployeeController()

{

}


[NonAction]

public Employee GetEmployee(int id)

{

    return employeeList.Where(s => s.EmployeeId ==
id).FirstOrDefault();

}

}
```

Remember that the MVC framework routing engine uses Action

Selectors attributes to determine the action method that is to be

invoked. The MVC 5 provides us with 3 action selector

attributes, which we have discussed. We use the ActionName

attribute to specify the name of the action other than the

method name. A NonAction attribute will mark the controller

class's public method as a non-action method. Note that this

cannot be invoked!

This type of selector should be used when you need to control selection of an action method depending on the Http request method. A good example is that you are allowed to define two different action methods having same name, but an action method usually responds to a HTTP Get request, then another action method will respond to a HTTP post request.

The MVC framework is capable of supporting different ActionVerbs like HttpGet, HttpPost, HttpDelete, HttpOptions , HttpPut, and HttpPatch. The attributes can be applied to the action method to indicate which Http requests the action method will support. If no attribute is applied, then the default setting is that this will be considered to be a GET request. Consider the example given below, which shows how different actions methods usually support the different ActionVerbs:

public class EmployeeController : Controller

{

```csharp
public ActionResult Index()
{
    return View();
}



[HttpPost]
public ActionResult PostAction()
{
    return View("Index");
}




[HttpPut]
public ActionResult PutAction()
{
    return View("Index");
}


[HttpDelete]
public ActionResult DeleteAction()
```

```csharp
{

    return View("Index");

}


[HttpHead]

public ActionResult HeadAction()

{

    return View("Index");

}


[HttpOptions]

public ActionResult OptionsAction()

{

    return View("Index");

}


[HttpPatch]

public ActionResult PatchAction()

{

    return View("Index");
```

```
    }

}
```

The "HttpPost" given in the above example supports the ActionPost as the action verb. The HttpDelete Action method supports the DeleteAction action verb. In short, the action verb is the one responsible for implementing the true activity of the action method. Multiple http verbs can also be applied using the AcceptVerbs attribute. The method GetAndPostAction is capable of supporting both the GET and the POST ActionVerbs, as shown in the example given below:

```
[AcceptVerbs(HttpVerbs.Post | HttpVerbs.Get)]
public ActionResult GetAndPostAction()
{
    return RedirectToAction("Index");
}
```

Before ending our discussion on this section, please note that ActionVerbs are simply other Action Selectors that choose an action method depending on the request methods such as GET, POST, PUT and others. Multiple action methods may have similar names but with different action verbs. It is also possible to apply different rules for method overloading. You can also apply multiple action verbs to a single action method using the AcceptVerbs attribute.

Chapter 5- Razor Syntax

Razor is a view engine supported in ASP.NET MVC. With it, you can mix your HTML code with a server side code such as Visual Basic or C#. When Razor view is used with Visual Basic, it has an extension of .vbhtml; when it is used with C#, it has an extension of .cshtml. The following are the characteristics of Razor Syntax:

1. Compact- Razor has a compact syntax that will allow you to minimize the number of characters as well as keystrokes that are required for the code to be written.

2. Easy to learn- Razor has an easy to learn syntax, since you are able to use the most basic languages such as Visual Basic and C#.

3. Intellisense- the Razor statements allows you to use auto-completion when programming in Visual Studio.

We can now go ahead and learn how Razor code is written.

Inline Expression

If you need to write a server side code for VB or C# with HTML, just begin with the @ symbol. A good example is @Variable_Name, which can be used for displaying the value of the server-side variable. The DateTime.Now usually gives the current date and time. If you need to show the current datetime, just write @DateTime.Now as it is shown below. Note that when you have written a single line expression, you don't need to add a semicolon at the end:

<h1>Razor syntax example</h1>

<h2>@DateTime.Now.ToShortDateString()</h2>

The code should print the current date on your system.

Multi-statement Code block

You can write multiple lines of code for the server side and then enclose them within @{ ... }. Each of these lines should end with a semicolon (;), as is the case in C#. This is shown below:

```
@{
    var date = DateTime.Now.ToShortDateString();
    var message = "Hello World";
}


<h2>Today is on: @date </h2>
<h3>@message</h3>
```

You will get the current date and the "Hello World" statement.

Displaying text from code block

To display text within a code block, you should use the @ symbol or <text>/<text>. The following example best demonstrates this:

```
@{
    var date = DateTime.Now.ToShortDateString();
    string message = "Hello World!";
    @:Today is on: @date <br />
    @message
}
```

Note the use of @ before the ": Today..." This helps us to display that text when we run the program. Let's demonstrate how we can use <text> </text> to display text within a code block:

```
@{
    var date = DateTime.Now.ToShortDateString();
```

```
    string message = "Hello World!";

    <text>Today is on:</text> @date <br />

    @message
}
```

As shown above, the text has been enclosed within <text> to mark the beginning of the text and </text> to mark the end of the text that is to be displayed on the screen once the program is run.

if-else condition

The "if-else" statement should be written beginning with the @ symbol. The code block for this statement has to be enclosed within the curly braces {}, even if it is a single statement. This is shown below:

```
@if(DateTime.IsLeapYear(DateTime.Now.Year) )
{
```

```
    @DateTime.Now.Year @:is a leap year.
}
else {
    @DateTime.Now.Year @:is not a leap year.
}
```

Note that the "if" part is executed first and then the "else" statement. Also note that the "if" part has to be evaluated for correctness. If it is found to be false, the execution will be taken to "else" part.

for loop

The "for" loop is used when we need to execute a set of statements or a single statement for a known number of times. You have to set the initial value for the loop, the increment amount, and the final value for the loop. This is demonstrated below:

```
@for (int x = 0; x < 5; x++) {

    @i.ToString() <br />

}
```

Once executed, you will get the following set of numbers:

```
0
1
2
3
4
```

Note that the initial value of the variable is 0, and its final value has to be less than 5. That's why you get values between 0 and 4.

Model

If you need to use a model object in your view, you should use the @model. Consider the example given below:

@model Student

```
<h2>Employee Details:</h2>
<ul>
   <li>Employee Id: @Model.EmployeeId</li>
   <li>Employee Name: @Model.EmployeeName</li>
   <li>Age: @Model.Age</li>
</ul>
```

The code will give you the details of the employee including the Employee ID, the Employee name, and the age.

Declaring Variables

A variable should be declared within a code block and enclosed within brackets, and the variables should be used within the html using the @ symbol. This is shown below:

```
@{
    string str = "";


    if(1 > 0)
    {
        str = "Hello World!";
    }
}


<p>@str</p>
```

Always remember that server-side code should be written using the @ symbol. This code should start with @{* code * }. If you need to display some text within your code block, just use the @ symbol or enclose the text within <text> and </text>. The if condition should begin within "@if{ }". If you need to add a model object to your view, just use the "@model".

Chapter 6- HTML Helpers

The Html helper class is responsible for generating html elements using model class objects in the razor view. It works by binding the model object to the html elements to display the value of the model properties into the html elements. It then assigns the value of the html elements to model properties when submitting the web form. You should always use the HtmlHelper class in the razor view rather than writing the html tags manually.

Creating a TextBox

We can use the HtmlHelper for the purpose of creating a TextBox. This class has two extension methods that can help us to create a textbox (<input type="text">) in the razor view: TextBox() and the TextBoxFor(). TextBox() is simply a loosely typed method, while the TextBoxFor() method is strongly typed. Let's use the Employee model for the purpose of demonstrating this. This is shown below:

```
public class Employee
{
    public int EmployeeId { get; set; }
    [Display(Name="Name")]
    public string EmployeeName { get; set; }
    public int Age { get; set; }
    public bool isNewlyEnrolled { get; set; }
    public string Password { get; set; }
}
```

Using "TextBox()"

The method "Html.TextBox()" usually creates the <input type="text" > element that has a specified name, value, and HTML attributes. The method takes the following signature:

MvcHtmlString Html.TextBox(string name, string value, object htmlAttributes)

There are many overloads for the TextBox() method. You can find them online. This method is loosely typed due to the fact that the parameter name is a string. This parameter can also be a property name for the model object. It works by binding the specified property within a textbox. This means that the value for the model property is displayed automatically on the textbox and vice versa. This is shown below:

@model Employee

@Html.TextBox("EmployeeName", null, new { @class = "form-control" })

The HTML result should be as shown below:

```
<input class="form-control"
    id="EmployeeName"
    name="EmployeeName"
    type="text"
    value="" />
```

In the example given above, "EmployeeName" forms the first parameter and this belongs to the Employee model class that has to be set as the name and the id for the textbox. The second parameter forms the value that will be displayed in the textbox, but in this case, it is null as the TextBox() method will show the value for the EmployeeName property in this textbox. Our third attribute has to be set as the class attribute.

The HtmlAttributes parameter is simply an object type and it may be an anonymous object, while the attributes name will be the properties that begin with the @ symbol. You can use the name that you want for the textbox. However, the binding to the model will not happen. The Html.TextBox() in Razor View should be as follows:

@Html.TextBox("txtBox", "This is value", new { @class = "form-control" })

The HTML Result for this will be as shown below:

<input class="form-control"

    id="txtBox"

    name="txtBox"

    type="text"

    value="This is value" />

This is value

The "TextBoxFor"

This is an extension method that is strongly typed. It usually generates some text input element for model property, which is specified by use of a lambda expression. The TextBoxFor method binds some specified model object property to an input text. This means it displays some value of model property automatically in the textbox and visa-versa. It takes the signature given below:

**MvcHtmlString
TextBoxFor(Expression<Func<TModel,TValue>>
expression, object htmlAttributes)**

Consider the example given below:

@model Employee

**@Html.TextBoxFor(m => m.EmployeeName, new {
@class = "form-control" })**

The HTML result for this will be as follows:

```
<input class="form-control"
    id="EmployeeName"
    name="EmployeeName"
    type="text"
    value="John" />
```

> John

In the example given above, the first parameter is in the form of a lambda expression and it has been used to specify the EmployeeName property that is to be bound with the textbox. It has to generate an input text element that has the id and the name that is set to the property name. The attribute "value" has to be set to the value of the EmployeeName property such as John.

The HtmlHelper class has two extension methods that can help us generate a multi line textarea in the razor view. These methods are TextArea() and the TextAreaFor(). The default setting is that it will create a textarea that has 2 rows and 20 columns. Let's use the Employee model to demonstrate this:

```
public class Employee
{
    public int EmployeeId { get; set; }
    [Display(Name="Name")]
    public string EmployeeName { get; set; }
    public string Description { get; set; }
}
```

Using "TextArea()" Method

The method "Html.TextArea()" creates a textarea of 2 rows and 20 columns, together with a specified name, html attributes, and value. It takes the signature given below:

MvcHtmlString Html.TextArea(string name, string value, object htmlAttributes)

This method is associated with many overloads. Since the parameter "name" is a string, this method is loosely typed. This parameter may be used as a property name for a model object. It works by binding some specified property with a textarea. This means that it displays a value of model property in the textarea and vice-versa. This is shown below:

@model Employee

@Html.TextArea("Desc", null, new { @class = "form-control" })

The HTML result should be as follows:

```
<textarea class="form-control"
    id="Desc"
    name="Desc"
    rows="2"
    cols="20">This is value</textarea>
```

In our example given above, we have the first property being the "Desc" of the Employee model class, and this will be used as the name and id of the textarea. Our second parameter forms the value that will be displayed in our textarea. In this example, this is null. Our third parameter is the class attribute. The textarea can be given the name that you want to use. However, binding to the model will not occur:

```
@Html.TextArea("txtArea", "This is value", new {
@class = "form-control" })
```

The HTML result should be as follows:

```
<textarea class="form-control"
    cols="20"
    id="txtArea"
    name="txtArea"
    rows="2">This is value</textarea>
```

The code should generate the output given below:

This is value

TextAreaFor

This is an extension method that is strongly typed. It usually generates a text input element for model property that is specified using a lambda expression. The TextAreaFor method binds some specified model object property to an input text. This means it displays a value of model property automatically in the textbox and vice-versa.The method takes the signature given below:

MvcHtmlString TextAreaFor(<Expression<Func<TModel,TValue>> expression, object htmlAttributes)

Consider the razor view example given below:

@model Employee

@Html.TextAreaFor(m => m.Desc, new { @class = "form-control" })

The HTML result for this should be as shown below:

```
<textarea class="form-control"
    cols="20"
    id="Desc"
    name="Desc"
    rows="2"></textarea>
```

In our example given above, the first parameter in the method TextAreaFor() method is a lambda expression specifying the model property that is to be bound with the textarea element. Note the use of the "Dec" property in the example. It will generate the <textarea> element that has an id and name that are set to the property name- Desc. That is why we have the value in the textarea set as the value for the Description property.

Creating a CheckBox

The HtmlHelper class has two extension methods that can be used for generation of <input type="checkbox"> element in the razor view. These methods are CheckBox() and the CheckBoxFor(). Let's use the Employee model to demonstrate how this works. Here is the Employee model:

```
public class Employee
{
    public int EmployeeId { get; set; }
    [Display(Name="Name")]
    public string EmployeeName { get; set; }
    public int Age { get; set; }
    public bool isNewlyEmployed { get; set; }
    public string Password { get; set; }
}
```

Using "CheckBox()" Method

The Html.CheckBox() method is loosely typed and it generates a <input type="checkbox" > that has a specified name, html attributes, and the isChecked Boolean. The method takes the following signature:

MvcHtmlString CheckBox(string name, bool isChecked, object htmlAttributes)

Consider the example given below:

@Html.CheckBox("isNewlyEnrolled", true)

The HTML result will be as shown below:

<input checked="checked"

    id="isNewlyEmployed"

    name="isNewlyEmployed"

    type="checkbox"

    value="true" />

In the example given above, the first parameter is the "isNewlyEmployed" property of Employee model class and it will be set as the name and id of the textbox. Our second parameter is a boolean value, for checking or unchecking the checkbox.

CheckBoxFor

This is a helper method that is strongly typed. It generates the element <input type="checkbox"> for a model property that is specified by use of a lambda expression. The CheckBoxFor method works by binding a specified model object property to the checkbox element. The checkbox is automatically checked or unchecked depending on the property value. The method takes the following signature:

MvcHtmlString CheckBoxFor(<Expression<Func<TModel,TValue>> expression, object htmlAttributes)

Consider the example given below:

@model Employee

@Html.CheckBoxFor(m => m.isNewlyEmployed)

The following is the code for the HTML result:

```
<input data-val="true"

    data-val-required="The isNewlyEmployed field is
required."

    id="isNewlyEmployed"

    name="isNewlyEmployed"

    type="checkbox"

    value="true" />
<input   name="isNewlyEmployed"   type="hidden"
value="false" />
```

In the example given above, the first parameter is "CheckBoxFor()"method, which is a lambda expression for specifying the model property that will be bound to the checkbox element. The "isNewlyEmployed" property has also been specified in the example. This will generate the <input type="checkbox"> element that has an id and name set to the property name, which is isNewlyEmployed. The value attribute will then be set to value of the isNewlyEmployed boolean property.

In the Html result given above, note that an additional hidden field has been generated with a similar name and the value=false. The reason for this is, once you submit the form with a checkbox, your value will only be posted if checkbox is checked. This means that if you leave your checkbox unchecked, there will be nothing to be sent to server during which, in many circumstances, you need a false to be sent. Since the hidden input has the same name as checkbox, if your checkbox is unchecked, then the server will still get a 'false'.

The HtmlHelper class also provides two methods that help to generate the <input type="radio"> element. These methods are RadioButton() and the RadioButtonFor(). We will again use our Employee model to demonstrate how these can be used:

```
public class Employee
{
    public int EmployeeId { get; set; }
    [Display(Name="Name")]
    public string StudentName { get; set; }
    public int Age { get; set; }
    public string Gender { get; set; }
}
```

Using "RadioButton()"

The method "Html.RadioButton()" creates a radio button element that have a specified name, html attributes, and the isChecked Boolean. The method takes the following signature:

MvcHtmlString RadioButton(string name, object value, bool isChecked, object htmlAttributes)

Consider the example given below, which shows how this can be used in the Razor view:

Male: @Html.RadioButton("Gender","Male")

Female: @Html.RadioButton("Gender","Female")

The HTML result for this will be as shown below:

Male: <input checked="checked"

id="Gender"

name="Gender"

type="radio"

value="Male" />

Female: <input id="Gender"

name="Gender"

type="radio"

value="Female" />

In the example given above, we have made two radio buttons for "Gender" property. Our second parameter is a value that will be sent to server, if the respective radio button has been checked. If the Male radio button has been selected, the string value "Male" will have to be assigned to the model property Gender and then submitted to server. The example creates two radio buttons, which are shown below.

Male:
Female:

RadioButtonFor

This is an extension method that is strongly typed. It generates the element "<input type="radio">" for property that has been specified using the Boolean expression. The method usually binds a specified model object property to a RadioButton control. The method takes the syntax given below:

MvcHtmlString RadioButtonFor(<Expression<Func<TModel,TValue >> expression, object value, object htmlAttributes)

Consider the example given below:

@model Employee

@Html.RadioButtonFor(m => m.Gender,"Male")

@Html.RadioButtonFor(m => m.Gender,"Female")

The HTML result for the above will be as shown below:

```
<input checked="checked"
    id="Gender"
    name="Gender"
    type="radio"
    value="Male" />

<input id="Gender"
    name="Gender"
    type="radio"
    value="Female" />
```

In the example given above, the first parameter in the RadioButtonFor() method is a lambda expression that specifies model property that is to be bound with the RadioButton element.

Two radio buttons have been created for Gender property in this example. This means that two <input type="RadioButton"> elements will be generated with id and name set to the property name, which is Gender. Our second parameter is the value that will be sent to the server once the form has been submitted.

Creating a DropDownList

The HtmlHelper class also provides us with two extension methods that generate the <select> element in the razor view. These methods are DropDownList() and the DropDownListFor(). We will use the Employee model given below to demonstrate how these methods can be used:

```
public class Employee
{
    public int EmployeeId { get; set; }
    [Display(Name="Name")]
    public string EmployeeName { get; set; }
    public Gender EmployeeGender { get; set; }
}
```

public enum Gender

{

    Male,

    Female

}

Using DropDownList()

The method Html.DropDownList() creates a <select> method that has a specified name, html attributes, and list items. The method takes the signature given below:

MvcHtmlString Html.DropDownList(string name, IEnumerable<SelectLestItem> selectList, string optionLabel, object htmlAttributes)

Consider the example given below:

@using MyMVCApp.Models

@model Employee

@Html.DropDownList("EmployeeGender",

    new SelectList(Enum.GetValues(typeof(Gender))),

    "Select Gender",

    new { @class = "form-control" })

The corresponding HTML result should be as shown below:

```
<select class="form-control" id="EmployeeGender" name="EmployeeGender">
    <option>Select Gender</option>
    <option>Male</option>
    <option>Female</option>
</select>
```

In the above example, the first parameter is a property name we need to display the list items for. The second parameter refers to a list of values that are to be included in dropdownlist. We made use of Enum methods to get the Gender enum values. Our third parameter is a label that will have to be the first list item, while our fourth parameter is for the html attributes such as css that are to be applied on dropdownlist.

Using "DropDownListFor"

This is an extension method that is strongly typed. It works by generating a <select> element for property that is specified using lambda expression. The method binds a model object property that is specified to a dropdownlist control. This means that it lists items automatically in the DropDownList depending on the property value. The method takes the signature given below:

MvcHtmlString Html.DropDownListFor(Expression<Func<dynamic, TProperty>> expression, IEnumerable<SelectLestItem> selectList, string optionLabel, object htmlAttributes)

Consider the example given below, which helps us create a dropdown for the Gender enum:


```
@using MyMVCApp.Models

@model Employee

@Html.DropDownListFor(m => m.EmployeeGender,

        new
SelectList(Enum.GetValues(typeof(Gender))),

        "Select Gender")
```


The HTML Result should be as shown below:


```
<select class="form-control" id="EmployeeGender"
name="EmployeeGender">

  <option>Select Gender</option>

  <option>Male</option>

  <option>Female</option>

</select>
```

In the example given above, the first parameter in the DropDownListFor() method is a lambda expression that specifies the model property that is to be bound with the select element. We have specified the EmployeeGender property of the enum type. Our second parameter specifies items to be shown in the dropdown list using SelectList. The third parameter is the optionLabel, which will be our first item in the dropdownlist. This will generate <select> element with an id and name set to the property name, which is EmployeeGender and the two list items, that is, Male and Female.

Gender: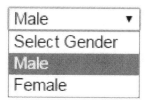

Creating a Password Field

The HtmlHelper class also comes with two extension methods that can help us create a password field in the razor view. These methods are Password() and the PasswordFor(). We will use the Employee model given below:

public class Employee

{

    public int Employee Id { get; set; }

    [Display(Name="Name")]

    public string EmployeeName { get; set; }

    public int Age { get; set; }

    public bool isNewlyEmployed { get; set; }

    public string OnlinePassword { get; set; }

}

Using "Password()"

The method Html.Password()generates an input password element that has a specified name, value, and the html attributes.The method takes the signature given below:

MvcHtmlString Html.Password(string name, object value, object htmlAttributes)

The method also has many overloads. Consider the example given below:

@model Employee

@Html.Password("OnlinePassword")

The HTML result for this should be as shown below:

<input

    id="OnlinePassword"

    name="OnlinePassword"

type="password"

value="" />

The code will then create a password field for you.

PasswordFor()

This is also a strongly typed helper method. It generates the element <input type="password"> for model object property that is specified using a lambda expression. The PasswordFor() method usually binds the specified model object property to the <input type="password">. This means that it sets a value of model property automatically to the password field and vice-versa.The method takes the signature given below:

**MvcHtmlString
Html.PasswordFor(Expression<Func<dynamic,TPro
perty>> expression, object htmlAttributes)**

Consider the example given below:

@model Employee

@Html.PasswordFor(m => m.Password)

The HTML Result should be as follows:

<input id="Password" name="Password" type="password" value="mpassword" />

In the example given above, our first parameter in the method PasswordFor() is a lambda expression that specifies model property hat is to bind with password textbox. We have also specified the Password property in our above example. This means that it will generate the input password element that has an id and name set to the property name. The value attribute will have to be set to value of the Password property and this is the "mpassword" in our example.

Chapter 7- Model Binding

Model binding helps a MVC framework to convert the values from an http request to parameters for an action method. The parameters can be of a complex or primitive type.

Binding to Primitive Type

The HttpGET request usually embeds data into a query string. The MVC framework converts a query string to action method parameters automatically.

You can have multiple parameters in an action method with the different data types. The query string values have to be converted into the parameters depending on the matching name. For example:

http://localhost/Employee/Edit?id=1&name=John

will be mapped to id and the name parameter of the Edit action method given below:

```
public ActionResult Edit(int id, string name)
{
    // add something here
        return View();
}
```

Binding to Complex Types

Model binding can also be applied to complex types. The model binding in the MVC framework will automatically convert the form field data of the Http request to properties of a complex type parameter of the action method.Consider the model class given below:

```
public class Employee
{
    public int EmployeeId { get; set; }
    [Display(Name="Name")]
    public string EmployeeName { get; set; }
```

```
    public int Age { get; set; }

    public Standard standard { get; set; }

}


public class Department

{

    public int DepartmentId { get; set; }

    public string DepartmentName { get; set; }

}
```

At this point, you can create an action method with the Employee type parameter. In the example given below, the Edit action method (the HttpPost) has Employee type parameter. This is shown below:

```
[HttpPost]

public ActionResult Edit(Employee emp)

{
```

```
        var id = emp.EmployeeId;

        var name = emp.EmployeeName;

        var age = emp.Age;

        var DepartmentName =
emp.department.DepartmentName;

        //update the database here..

        return RedirectToAction("Index");
}
```

The MVC framework will map the Form collection values
automatically to the Employee type parameter once the form
has submitted the http POST request to the Edit action method.

Bind Attribute

The ASP.NET MVC framework enables you to specify the properties of the model class that needs to be bound. The [Bind] attribute will allow you to specify the exact properties that a model binder has to include or exclude in the binding.

In the example given below, the Edit action method only has the bind EmployeeName and EmployeeName property of the Employee model. This is shown below:

```
[HttpPost]
public ActionResult Edit([Bind(Include =
"EmployeeId, EmployeeName")] Employee emp)

{

    var name = emp.EmployeeName;


    //write code for updating employee


    return RedirectToAction("Index");
```

```
}
```

The properties can also be excluded as shown below:

```
[HttpPost]
public ActionResult Edit([Bind(Exclude = "Age")]
Employee emp)
{
    var name = emp.EmployeeName;
    //write code for updating employee
      return RedirectToAction("Index");
}
```

The Bind attribute is responsible for improving the performance only by the bind properties that are needed.

Chapter 8- ViewData

The ViewData tool is useful when you need to transfer data from the Controller to the View. The ViewData is simply a dictionary that may have key-value pairs in which each key is a string. The ViewData will only transfer data from the controller to the view, not vice-versa. It only becomes valid during current asset. Consider the example given below, which shows how data can be transferred from the controller to view:

```
public ActionResult Index()
{
    IList<Employee> employeeList = new List<Employee>();

    employeeList.Add(new Employee(){
EmployeeName = "John" });

    employeeList.Add(new Employee(){
EmployeeName = "Steve" });

    employeeList.Add(new Employee(){
EmployeeName = "Hillary" });

    ViewData["employees"] = employeeList;
```

```
    return View();

}
```

In the example given above, we have just added the employee list with key "employees" in ViewData dictionary. It is now possible for us to access the employee list as shown below:

```
<ul>

@foreach (var emp in ViewData["employees"] as
IList<Employee>)

{

  <li>

    @emp.EmployeeName

  </li>

}

</ul>
```

Note that the ViewData values can be casted to appropriate data type. The KeyValuePair can then be added into the ViewData as shown below:

```csharp
public ActionResult Index()

{

    ViewData.Add("Id", 1);

    ViewData.Add(new KeyValuePair<string,
object>("Name", "John"));

    ViewData.Add(new KeyValuePair<string,
object>("Age", 21));

    return View();

}
```

The ViewBag and ViewData both have an internal dictionary. This means that you can't have the ViewData key matching with the property name of the ViewBag. Otherwise, an exception will be thrown. This is shown below:

```csharp
public ActionResult Index()

{

    ViewBag.Id = 1;

    ViewData.Add("Id", 1);
```

```
   // throw the runtime exception as it now has a "Id"
key

   ViewData.Add(new KeyValuePair<string,
object>("Name", "John"));

   ViewData.Add(new KeyValuePair<string,
object>("Age", 21));

   return View();

}
```

The ViewData usually transfers data from the Controller to the View, but the opposite is not true. It is derived from ViewDataDictionary, which is simply a dictionary type. It only remains valid during the current http request. Its values are usually lost once a redirection occurs. Before you can use a ViewData value, you should first type cast it. The ViewBag will insert the data internally into the ViewBag dictionary. This is why the property for ViewBag and the key for ViewData should not match.

Chapter 9- Filters

A filter is a custom class in which you can write a custom logic that is to be executed before or after the action method has been executed. They can be applied to the action method or to the controller programmatically or declaratively. Consider the example given below; which shows the HandErrorAttribute that is a built-in exception filter:

[HandleError]

public class HomeController : Controller

{

   public ActionResult Index()

   {

     //throw and exception

     throw new Exception("This is an unhandled exception");

     return View();

   }

```
public ActionResult About()

{

    return View();

}


public ActionResult Contact()

{

    return View();

}

}
```

In the example given above, the [HandleError] attribute has been applied to the HomeController. This means that an error page will be displayed once any action method for the HomeController throws an unhandled exception. Note that unhandled exception refers to the exception that cannot be handled by a try-catch block.

Always remember to put on the custom mode in the System.web

section of the we.config. This is shown below:

<customErrors mode="On" />

After running the app, you should get an error page since the

exception is thrown in the Index action method.

Register Filters

There are three levels in which filters can be applied:

Global Level

Filters may be applied at the global level in the

Application_Start event of the file Global.asax.cs using the

default FilterConfig.RegisterGlobalFilters() method. The

example given below shows the [HandleError] that is used by

default in all MVC applications:

```csharp
// MvcApplication class is in the Global.asax.cs file


public class MvcApplication :
System.Web.HttpApplication
{

    protected void Application_Start()

    {


FilterConfig.RegisterGlobalFilters(GlobalFilters.Filters);

    }

}
// FilterConfig.cs located in App_Start folder

public class FilterConfig

{

    public static void
RegisterGlobalFilters(GlobalFilterCollection filters)

    {

        filters.Add(new HandleErrorAttribute());

    }
```

Controller level

It is also possible to apply filters to the controller class. The following example demonstrates this:

```
[HandleError]
public class HomeController : Controller
{
    public ActionResult Index()
    {
        return View();
    }
}
```

Filters an also be applied on an individual action method. After that, the filter will only be applicable to that method:

```
public class HomeController : Controller
{
    [HandleError]
    public ActionResult Index()
    {
        return View();
    }
}
```

Chapter 10- Adding a Controller

The aim of using MVC (Mode-View-Controller) in development is to create applications which are easy to test, maintain, and with a good architecture.

We need to begin by creating a controller class. Just click on *"Solution Explorer"* and then choose *"Add"*. Select *"Controller"*.

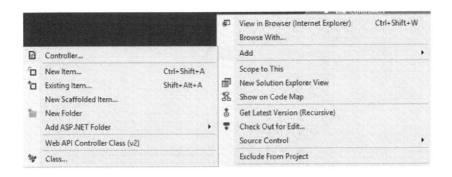

A dialog will appear, which is an "Add *Scaffold*" dialog. Just choose *"MVC 5 Controller- Empty"* and then select *"Add"*.

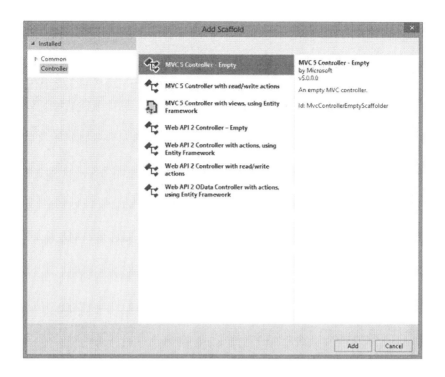

In the next dialog which will appear, you will be prompted to provide a name for your controller, just do that and then click on the *"Add"* button. If you check keenly on the *"Solution Explorer"*, you will notice that a new file has been created with the name that you specified for your controller. A new folder will also be created. The controller will be opened in the IDE as shown below:

```csharp
using System;
using System.Collections.Generic;
using System.Linq;
using System.Web;
using System.Web.Mvc;

namespace MvcMovie.Controllers
{
    0 references
    public class HelloWorldController : Controller
    {
        //
        // GET: /HelloWorld/
        0 references
        public ActionResult Index()
        {
            return View();
        }
    }
}
```

We now need to write our first ASP.NET MVC 5 code. Just replace the above default code with the following code:

using System.Web;

using System.Web.Mvc;

namespace FirstApp.Controllers

{

```
public class FirstApp : Controller
{
    //
    // GET: /FirstApp/
    public string Index()
    {
        return "Hello there! <b>welcome</b> to
        ASP.NETMVC 5...";
    }
    //
    // GET: /FirstApp/Welcome/
    public string Hello()
    {
        return "This is our first ASP.NET application, hope
        you enjoy...";
    }
}
```

Just write the above program in your IDE. Once you are through, run it by pressing the "*F5*" key on your keyboard. You will notice that your browser will be opened and the following will be displayed as the output:

Hello there! **welcome** to ASP.NETMVC 5...

What happened in our code is that we began by importing the necessary modules to our program. To import a module or a library in ASP.NET, we use the "using" keyword.

This keyword is then followed by the name of the module that needs to be imported. To define a class in ASP.NET, we use the "class" keyword, which can be preceded by the type of the class.

The type can be either public or private. The "return" statement is used in Asp.net for printing text on the screen. Also, we have defined a function named "Hello()".

The brackets () indicate that we are creating a function, as that is how a function is denoted in asp.net. This function is of the public type and it takes a data of type string.

With ASP.NET, different classes can be invoked. It depends with the URL which is upcoming. Note that there is a default URL format for this in ASP.NET.

The routing format is set in the file "app_start/routeconfig.cs" which is shown below:

```
public static void RegisterRoutes(RouteCollection routes)
{
routes.IgnoreRoute("{resource}.axd/{*pathInfo}");

routes.MapRoute(

name: "Default",

url: "{controller}/{action}/{id}",

defaults: new { controller = "Home", action = "Index", id = UrlParameter.Optional }

);

}
```

In this example, we have a method named "RegisterRouters), which takes the parameter "routes" of type "RouteCollection". The parameter "routes" has then been used in the rest of the program code as the actions are to be performed on the routes that are passed.

Whenever the application is run without having specified the URL the default page will be opened. The first part of your URL will be responsible for determining the kind of view which will be executed. The second part is responsible for determining the kind of action method which will be executed.

 If there is no method specified, then the default "*index*" method will be called. At this time, we will not say much about the third part of the URL but just know that it is for route data.

We need to see the effect of running the action method, that is, "*Hello()*", which we created. Just open it in your browser. The following will be observed as the output:

This is our first ASP.NET application, hope you enjoy...

We now need to modify the previous example so as to include some parameters in the method. The *"Hello()"* method will be modified to accommodate only two parameters as it is shown below:

public string Hello(string name, int numTimes = 1) {

return HttpUtility.HtmlEncode("Hi " + name + ", the NumTimes is: " + numTimes);

}

Our "Hello()" method has been modified to take the argument's "name" and "numtimes". The name parameter is of type string, while the other one will take an integer data type.

You can see how parameter passing is done in Asp.net from the line that begins with the "return" statement. The Hello() method should be called while specifying the values of the parameters and it will print the necessary output.

Note that the "Index()" is the default one that has to be called once a controller has been specified explicitly. The "Hello()" should run and then return the string below it because it forms the action method in our case. The numTimes parameter will take a default value of 1 if you don't pass a parameter to it.

Note that in the above code, we have borrowed a C# feature for the purpose of indicating that the above parameter should default to 1 in case the programmer passes no value to the parameter.

You can now run your application again after the above changes. You can try different values for the parameters and see what will happen. To run this program, you just have to open the URL given below:

http://localhost:xxxx/FirstApp/Hello?name=Kira&nu

mtimes=4)

Note that we have passed the value "Kira" to the parameter name and 4 to the parameter numTimes.

The mapping of the parameters from the query string in your address bar to the method will be done effectively. The following shows a sample output after adding the parameters:

Hi Kira, the NumTimes is 4

In the example above, we have passed the two parameters as query strings. We have the symbol (?), that is, a question mark which should act as a separator.

This separates the name of the action method from its respective parameters. This is then followed by the query strings. Try to replace the *"Hello()"* method with the following code:

```
public string Hello(string name, int id = 1)
{
return HttpUtility.HtmlEncode("Hi " + name + ", the id is: " + id);
```

Once you have written the above code, just run it by supplying the necessary URL to the browser. The URL should be specified as follows:

http://localhost:xxx/FirstApp/Hello/3?name=Kira

You should observe the following as the output:

Hi Kira, the id is 3

The route ID and the third part of the URL matched. It is shown in the above figure that the value of the "*id*" is 3. We have used the parameter "*id*" in the "*Hello()*" method. This matched the specification of the URL in the method "*RegisterRoutes*". This is shown in the c# code given below:

```csharp
public static void RegisterRoutes(RouteCollection routes)
{
routes.IgnoreRoute("{resource}.axd/{*pathInfo}");

routes.MapRoute(

name: "Default",

url: "{controller}/{action}/{id}",

defaults: new { controller = "Home", action = "Index", id = UrlParameter.Optional }

);
}
```

If you are programming ASP.NET MVC applications, it is highly recommended that parameters should be passed in as route data rather than as query strings.

It is possible for the *"name"* and the *"numTimes"* to be passed in as route data in your URL by adding a route. This can be done as follows:

```
public class RouteConfig
{
public static void RegisterRoutes(RouteCollection routes)
{
routes.IgnoreRoute("{resource}.axd/{*pathInfo}");
routes.MapRoute(
name: "Default",
url: "{controller}/{action}/{id}",
defaults: new { controller = "Home", action = "Index", id = UrlParameter.Optional }
);
routes.MapRoute(
name: "Welcome",
url: "{controller}/{action}/{name}/{id}"
);
}
}}
```

Just do as we have done in the above sample program. To run the application, just open the following URL on the browser:

/localhost:XXX/FirstApp/Hello/Kira/3

After running it, you will observe the following output:

Hi Kira, the id is 3

The default route will work efficiently in most MVC applications. The model binder is also another way on how this can be done, whereby you will not be required to modify the default route.

Chapter 11- Adding a View

In the previous chapter, the controllers which we created served the work of both the views and the controllers. We have used the controller to directly return HTML. When controllers are used for returning HTML, the code becomes too cumbersome. In this chapter, you will learn how to create a view template and then use it for generation of the HTML response.

This will be done using the Razor view engine. Files containing the view template made using Razor view engine usually have a *".cshtml"* extension in their name. It makes it possible for programmers to create view templates in a much easier and faster way. Consider the code shown below:

public ActionResult Index()

{

return View();

}

What we have done in the above code is that we have changed the *"Index()"* method so that it can return a view object. This is contrary to the previous examples in which the returned result was a string message which was hard coded in the controller class. The *"Index()"* method is responsible for generation of an HTML response to the browser by use of a view template. Controller methods will always return an *"ActionResult"*.

Open your IDE and right click on *"views/FirstApp"* folder. Choose *"Add"* and then click on *"MVC 5 view page with (Layout Razor)"*. This is shown in the figure below:

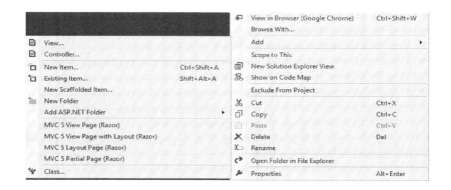

A dialog with the title *"Specify Name for Item"* will appear. Provide the name *"Index"*. After that, just click on the *"ok"* button. The next dialog to appear will have the title *"Select a Layout Page"*. Select *"_Layout.cshtml"* and then click on the *"ok"* button.

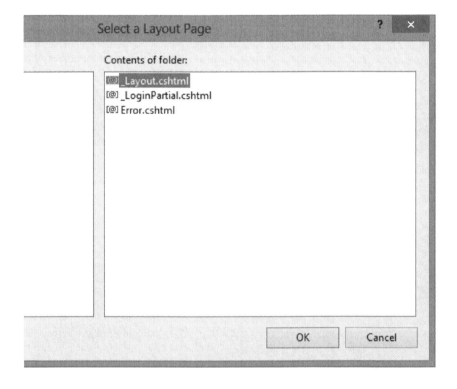

Your file will have been created. In the above folder, you have also noticed the *"shared"* folder under *"view"* to the left of the dialog is selected by default. In case you had created a custom layout file in just another folder, then select it.

You then need to add the following code:

```
@{

Layout = "~/Views/Shared/_Layout.cshtml";

}

@{

ViewBag.Title = "Index";

}

<h2>Index file</h2>

<p>Hello, this is our view template!</p>
```

In the *"Solution Explorer"* window, right click the

"Index.cshtml" file and then choose *"View in Browser"*.

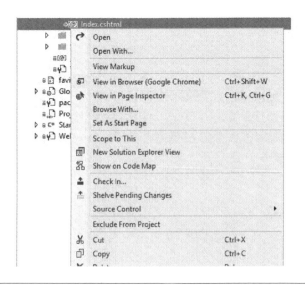

If you are not comfortable with this method, just right click on the file *"Index.cshtml"* and then choose *"View in Page Inspector"*. It is possible that you open the browser and then use it to navigate to the *"FirstApp"* controller. The index method is responsible for running the *"return view()"* statement which specifies that the above method should provide a response to the browser by use of a view template. Note that we did not specify the kind of view template that the method should use.

Due to this, ASP.NET MVC 5 will use the default view, which is the *"index.cshtml"* located in the folder *"\views\FirstApp"*. Open the browser and then navigate to the FirstApp controller. Just type the URL given below:

http://localhost:xxxx/FirstApp

Consider the following figure showing the output after running the program:

Hello, this is our view template!

Notice that the above output shows what we coded in our view rather than in our controller. This is in contrast to what we did in our previous chapter.

In case you need to see the links which we mentioned earlier, you might need to click on the menu icon located at the right of the browser. However, this will depend on the size of the browser.

How to change the Views and Layout Pages

You should start by changing the link *"Application name"* located at the top of the page. This link will be seen on every page of the application, but its implementation is only done in a single place in your application.

Click on the *"Solutions Explorer"* and then open the *"/views/shared"* folder. Open the file *"_.Layout.cshtml"*. This file is the one responsible for providing layout to your application and it is shared by all the pages of your application.

With the layout templates, the programmer is able to specify the lookout of the HTML container for the website. Once this container has been specified, then all the pages of the website can make use of it, meaning that the work of development will have been made much simpler.

It is in this layout file that you will find the *"Renderbody()"* function which is a placeholder responsible for showing all the pages of your web application.

A good example is when you select the *"Contact"* link. The view *"Views\Home\Contact.cshtml"* will be rendered inside this function. The complete layout files should be as follows:

```html
<!DOCTYPE html>

<html>

<head>

<meta charset="utf-8" />

<meta name="viewport" content="width=device-
width, initial-scale=1.0">

<title>@ViewBag.Title – First App</title>

@Styles.Render("~/Content/css")

@Scripts.Render("~/bundles/modernizr")

</head>

<body>

<div class="navbar navbar-inverse navbar-fixed-
top">

<div class="container">

<div class="navbar-header">

<button type="button" class="navbar-toggle" data-
toggle="collapse" data-target=".navbar-collapse">

<span class="icon-bar"></span>

<span class="icon-bar"></span>

<span class="icon-bar"></span>

</button>
```

```
@Html.ActionLink("First App", "Index", "First", null,
new { @class = "navbar-brand" })

</div>

<div class="navbar-collapse collapse">

<ul class="nav navbar-nav">

<li>@Html.ActionLink("Home", "Index",
"Home")</li>

<li>@Html.ActionLink("About", "About",
"Home")</li>

<li>@Html.ActionLink("Contact", "Contact",
"Home")</li>

</ul>

@Html.Partial("_LoginPartial")

</div>

</div>

</div>

<div class="container body-content">

@RenderBody()

<hr />

<footer>

<p>&copy; @DateTime.Now.Year - My ASP.NET
Application</p>
```

```
</footer>

</div>


@Scripts.Render("~/bundles/jquery")

@Scripts.Render("~/bundles/bootstrap")

@RenderSection("scripts", required: false)

</body>

</html>
```

Just modify the layout file until it is as shown in the above code. Note that the change was only made in the template file once, and now all the pages that are on the site are capable of reflecting this new change. Once you are through, just run it and observe the output. It will be as follows:

The modification worked successfully. To demonstrate is on whether we added an event to our layout page, click on the "*About*" link. The following window will appear:

About.

Your application description page.

Use this area to provide additional information.

© 2013 - My ASP.NET Application

You will also notice that "*First App*" will show on each of the web pages. Remember that we said the purpose of a layout template is to make the pages of your web application uniform. This shows that we achieved it, hence an advancement. All the pages of the site have reflected the changes we have implemented.

The first time after creation of the

"Views\FirstApp\Index.cshtml" file, we only had the following

code:


```
@{
Layout = "~/Views/Shared/_Layout.cshtml";
}
```


This is what defined the appearance of our web pages, and it is

the Razor. Notice the use of the "Layout" keyword, which shows

how the web page will appear once we open it. The

"Views/ViewStart.cshtml" file will have the same Razor

markup.

This file defines the layout that the views of your web

application should take. This means that it is the view that is

common to all our web pages and they should use it in forming

the layout. This means that this cannot be deleted or

commented in the *"Index.htl"* file.

```
@*@{

Layout = "~/Views/Shared/_Layout.cshtml";

}*@

@{

ViewBag.Title = "Index";

}

<h2>Index file</h2>

<p> Hello, this is our view template! </p>\
```

Note that the layout for the webpage has been set using the "Layout" keyword. We have also set a header (<h2>) and a paragraph(<p>). If you do not need to use any layout, just set it to "*null*" or just remove it. Also, if you want to use another layout, you are free to change this.

We now need to change the title of our Index view. To do this, open the "*Index.cshtml*" file. We need to change the value of the text which forms the title in our browser and the "*h2*" element, which forms the secondary header.

You have to make them somehow different so as to observe the change in your app.

```
@{
ViewBag.Title = "First App";
}
<h2>My First Application</h2>
<p> Hello, this is our view template! </p>
```

The underlined elements are the ones which need to be changed. We now need to change the HTML title that will be displayed. The above code enabled us to change the *"title"* property of the object *"viewBag"*. Consider the code given below:

```
<!DOCTYPE html>
<html>
<head>
<meta charset="utf-8" />
```

```
<meta   name="viewport"   content="width=device-width, initial-scale=1.0">
```

```
<title>@ViewBag.Title - First App</title>
```

```
@Styles.Render("~/Content/css")
```

```
@Scripts.Render("~/bundles/modernizr")
```

```
</head>
```

Note that to set the title for our app, we have used the "Title" element that belongs to the "ViewBag" object located in Index.cshtml view template. Note that our layout template, which is "Views\Shared_Layout.cshtml", makes use of this value in the <title> element to be part of <head> section of HTML, which has been modified previously. The *"viewBag"* approach makes it possible for you to pass data between the layout file and your view template.

You can now run the application and then observe the changes which have occurred. The title of the browser, the primary, and the secondary headings will all have changed. In case you fail to see these changes, then the current content being viewed might be the cached one. Reload the web page by pressing *"Ctrl + F5"* on your keyboard.The title displayed in the browser should be as shown below:

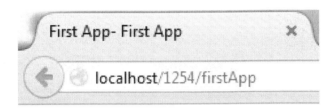

However, the links which were present by default will not be affected in any way. They remain as follows:

On the previous page which we had, you will notice the title, which is the secondary one has changed to the following:

My First App

Hello, this is our view template!

This shows that the changes which we implemented have taken effect, which is good. However, the text shown above, that is, *"Hello, this is our view template!"* has been hard-coded. In the next chapters, you will be able to retrieve this from somewhere else, particularly the model.

How to pass data from the Controller to the Viewer

It is good for you to know how to pass data to the viewer from the controller. Invocation of controller classes usually happens as a result of an incoming URL request which needs a response. The code which is responsible for handling requests from the objects of the browser should be implemented in the controller class.

If a database is involved, then the controller class is also responsible for accessing it and then retrieving data. It then decides on how to relay the response to the browser object.

The programmer can choose to use the view templates for rendering the response to the user. This can be done from the controller class. The main logic is carried out in the controller class. The objects necessary for the view to render the response on the browser are provided by the controller.

While programming in ASP.NET MVC 5, you should take advantage of the property *"separation of concerns"*. In this case, the view should not communicate directly with the model (database) but instead, it should always communicate with the controller. This idea makes programming a bit easier and the code will be easy to test.

We now need to work with our previous *"Hello()"* method. We want to render the output as a view template rather than as a string.

Just open the controller having this method and then change it to include the *"name"* and the *"numTimes"* to a viewBag object. The code should be as follows:

```csharp
using System.Web;

using System.Web.Mvc;

namespace FirstApp.Controllers

{

public class FirstAppController : Controller

{

public ActionResult Index()

{

return View();

}

public ActionResult Hello(string name, int numTimes = 1)

{

ViewBag.Message = "Hi " + name;

ViewBag.NumTimes = numTimes;

return View();

}

}

}
```

With the above code, the data to be passed directly to the view

is contained in the *"viewBag"* object. The next thing we need is

the view template for Hello.

Click on *"Build"* and then choose *"Build Solution"* or just press

"Ctrl + Shift + B". This will compile the project. Right click the

folder *"Views\FirstApp"* and then choose *"Add"*. Choose *"MVC*

5 View Page with (Layout Razor)".

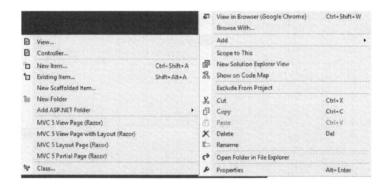

A dialog box will appear with the title *"Specify Name for the Item"*. Enter *"Hello"* as the name and then click on the *"ok"* button. A dialog will appear which will prompt you to select the layout page. Just accept the default one, which is *"_Layout.cshtml"*. Click on the *"ok"* button.

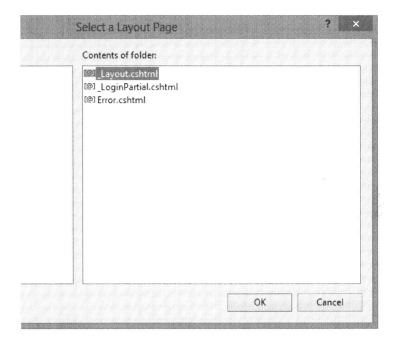

You will have created a file named *"Hello.cshtml"*. Replace the code in this with the following code:

```
@{

ViewBag.Title = "Hello";

}

<h2>Hello</h2>

<ul>

@for (int j = 0; j < ViewBag.NumTimes; j++)

{

<li>@ViewBag.Message</li>

}

</ul>
```

You can now run the app and then open the URL given below in your browser:

http://localhost:xx/FirstApp/Hello?name=Kira&num times=4

We have just created a loop which will print *"Hello"* on the screen as many times as the user specifies. The application is now ready, so you can run it. The controller is responsible for packaging data into a *"viewBag"* and it then passes it to the view.

Now data is being taken from the URL and then passed to a controller using a model binder. The controller will then package the data into a ViewBag object, and then pass the object to a view. This view will then render the data to the user in the form of HTML. That's how a ViewBag object can be used for passing data from a controller to a view.

Chapter 12- Adding a Model

We need to add some classes to the database. These classes will form the model of your application. An entity framework will be used for the purpose of defining and working with the classes.

How to add model classes

Open the "*Solutions Explorer*". Right click it and choose "*Add*". Select "*Class*".

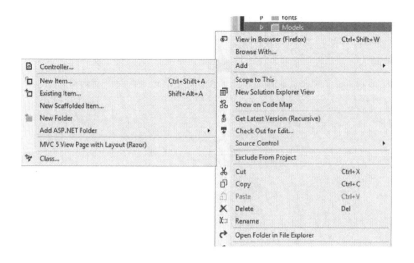

Provide the class name. I have given my class the name *"App"*.

Add the following code to the class:

```
using System;
namespace FirstApp.Models
{
public class App
{
public int id { get; set; }
public string Title { get; set; }
public DateTime DevelopmentDate { get; set; }
public string Area { get; set; }
public decimal Price { get; set; }
}
}
```

The above class will represent the data that we store in our database. **We have created a class named "App".**

Each instance of the class *"App"*, that is, an object, will correspond to one of the rows contained in the tables of the database. Each property in the class will represent a column in the tables of the database. In the same file, just add the code given below for *"AppDBContext"* class. Add the following code to the file:

```
using System;
using System.Data.Entity;
namespace FirstApp.Models
{
public class App
{
public int id { get; set; }
public string Title { get; set; }
public DateTime DevelopmentDate { get; set; }
public string Area { get; set; }
public decimal Price { get; set; }
}
```

```
public class AppDBContext : DbContext
{
public DbSet<App> FirstApp { get; set; }
}
}
```

The class "*AppDBContext*" will act as a representative of the EF
(Entity Framework) App database context. This is responsible
for fetching storing and updating the instances of the class
"*App*" in the database. "*AppDBContext*" is derived from
"*DBContext*" which is a base class and it is provided by the EF.
If you need to reference "*DbSet*" and "*DbContext*", the following
should be included at the top of the file:

```
using System.Data.Entity;
```

The above line can be added manually by typing. However, if
you can't manage to do that, a red line will be used to underline
where an error occurs.

Just right click on this line, choose *"Resolve"* and then choose

the above line as shown in the figure below:

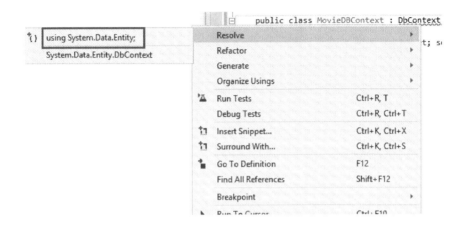

If you want to remove an unused statements with the keyword

"using", just right click the file, choose *"Organize strings"* and

then select *"Remove unused Usings"*. You have now added the

model to your application.

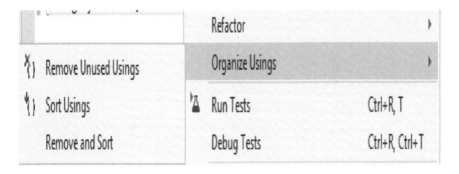

Chapter 13-Accessing data in the Model from the Controller

We want to create a class that will retrieve data from the model and then display it in the browser using a view template. Begin by building the application to avoid getting an error while adding a controller. Open the *"Solutions Explorer"* and right click on the folder written *"Controller"*. Choose *"Add"* then select *"Controller"*.

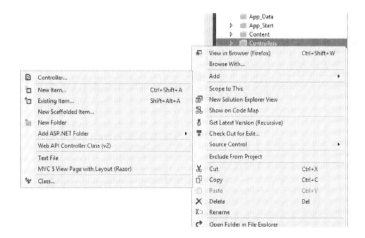

A dialog box with the title *"Add Scaffold"* will appear. Click on *"MVC 5 with views, using Entity Framework"*. Select *"Add"*.

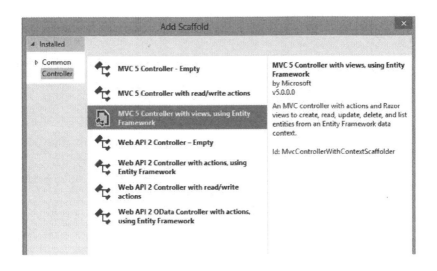

Provide "*AppController*" as the name of the controller. For the model class, choose "*App (FirstApp.Models)*". For the data context class, choose "*AppDBContext(FirstApp.Models)*". Click on the "*Add*" button. In case you get an error, this shows that you did not build the application as we said at the beginning of this chapter.

The following files will be created by visual studio:

- A *AppsController.cs* file contained in the *Controllers* folder.
- A *"Views\Movies"* folder.
- *"Create.cshtml"*, *"Delete.cshtml"*, *"Details.cshtml"*, *"Edit.cshtml"*, and *"Index.cshtml"* contained in the *"Views\Movies"* folder.

Visual studio automatically does what is called *"scaffolding"* for you, in which it creates *"CRUD* (create, read, update, and delete)" methods. Views will also be created automatically for you. Your web application is now fully functional. You can create, edit, list and even delete data from the web.

You can then run the application and browse to the Apps controller. This can be done by appending a /Apps to the URL to be opened in the browser.

The request http://localhost:xxxxx/Apps of the browser will be routed to the "Index" action method, which is the default of our Apps controller.

This means that the "http://localhost:xxxxx/Apps" browser request is just the same as the **"http://localhost:xxxxx/Apps/Index"** browser request. Since you don't have any application as data for the database, the result will be empty but it will just show the columns that we created. This is shown in the figure below:

My First App

Index

create new

Title DevelopmentDate Area Price

We now want to enter a new application to the database. This can be done with a great deal of ease. Just click on the link written "*create new*" as shown in the figure above. An interface will appear in which you will be required to provide the details of the application. The details are just the columns which we specified as shown in the figure above. Just do that and then click on the "*create*" button.

After clicking on the button shown in the above figure, the information that you provided will be posted to the server, and the details of the application will be saved into the database. The application will then guide you to the "*/Apps*" URL whereby you will be able to see the details of the apps which you have just provided. This is shown in the figure below:

My First App

Index

create new

Title DevelopmentDate Area Price

MyApp 12/06/2015 13:00:00 Computing 4

Besides the details of the app, there will be other options which can allow you to do something to the app. These are as follows:

Edit | Details | Delete

You can try to add details of other apps to the database as we have done with the above application. Also, try to edit and delete these details and observe what will happen. We now need to examine the code which has been generated. Just open the class "*Controllers\AppsController.cs*".

Observe the Index method which has been generated. You can find this at CONTROLLERS\APPSCONTROLLER.CS. A portion of this will be as shown below:

public class AppsController : Controller

{

private AppDBContext db = new AppDBContext();

// GET: /Applications/

public ActionResult Index()

{

return View(db.Apps.ToList());

}

If a request is sent to the "*Apps*" controller, the "*Apps*" table will be queried and all the Apps entered to this table will be returned to the "*Index*" view. Consider the line of code shown below:

private AppDBContext db = new AppDBContext();

The line is responsible for instantiation of the App database context. This instance can then be use to query, edit or even delete apps from the database.

Connecting to the SQL Server LocalDB

Code First, which is a feature in Entity Framework, detected that we were trying to establish a connection to a database which is not existing, so it created this database automatically. To confirm whether this happened, open the b"*App_data*" folder.

Check to see whether there is a file with the name "*Apps.mdf*". In case you do not find it, open the "*Solutions Explorer*" and click on "*Show All Files*". Refresh by clicking on the "*Refresh*" button and then expand the folder.

If you find the file "*Apps.mdf*", double click on it so as to open the "*SERVER EXPLORER*". Expand the folder containing tables so as to see the Apps tables.

You will notice that there is an icon beside the "id". This is a primary key which has been made automatically.

We now need to see the data that we entered. Just right click on the "*Apps*" table, and then select "*Show Table Data*".

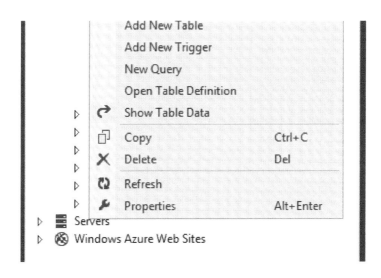

This will display the details of the apps which you have added into the database. We now need to see the structure of our table. Right click the table *"Apps"* and then select *"Open Table Definition"*. The structure of the table which the Entity Framework created for you will be displayed.

Now you are done with the database. You should now close it. Right click the *"AppDBContext"* and then choose *"Close Connection"*. This will close the connection. In case you fail to do this, then you might get an error if you run the application the next time.

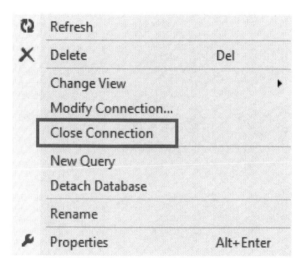

Chapter 14- Creating a Search Method

Let us create a search method which will be able to search for applications by using area and name. Open the *"AppsController"* class and update the *"Index"* method to be as follows:

public ActionResult Index(string sString)

{

var apps = from n in db.Apps

select n;

if (!String.IsNullOrEmpty(sString))

{

apps = apps.Where(s => s.Title.Contains(sString));

}

return View(apps);

}

The following query which is responsible for selecting the app from the database will be created by the first line of the above code:

var apps = from n in db.Apps

select n;

Note that we have used a "sString" to represent the title of the app as stored in the database. This means that we will search using the title of the app. At the above point, the query will be ready, but we have not run it against the database.

In case the parameter *"sString"* has a string, then the query *"apps"* will be modified so that it can filter the value of the search string. The following code will be used:

if (!String.IsNullOrEmpty(sString))

{

apps = apps.Where(s => s.Title.Contains(sString));

}

Notice the use of the code "*s -> s.Title*", which is a lambda expression. The "*Index*" view.], which is responsible for rendering the HTML to the user can now be modified. Just run the application to observe the output. The filtered apps will be as shown below:

My First App

Index

create new

Title DevelopmentDate Area Price

MyApp 12/06/2015 13:00:00 Computing 4

SecondApp 12/06/2015 14:00:00 Business 3

In case the signature of the "*Index*" method is changed, so that it can have parameter named "*id*", this will match the placeholder "*{id}*" for default routes. This is usually set in the file "*App_start/RouteConfig.cs*". The original Index file should be as follows:

```
public ActionResult Index(string sString)

{

var apps = from n in db.Apps

select n;

if (!String.IsNullOrEmpty(sString))

{

apps = apps.Where(s => s.Title.Contains(sString));

}

return View(apps);

}
```

After modifying it, it will be as follows:

```
public ActionResult Index(string id)

{

string sString = id;

var apps = from n in db.Apps

select n;

if (!String.IsNullOrEmpty(sString))

{
```

```
apps = apps.Where(s => s.Title.Contains(sString));
}
return View(apps);
}
```

The search title can now be passed as route data as opposed to a query string. However, it is not possible for users to modify the URL when they need to search for a new app from the database. It is also possible to add a user interface which will help the users to filter the apps. Consider the following code:

```
public ActionResult Index(string sString)
{
var apps = from n in db.Apps
select n;
if (!String.IsNullOrEmpty(sString))
{
apps = apps.Where(s => s.Title.Contains(sString));
}
return View(apps);
}
```

In the above code, we have changed the signature to test the passing of the route-bound ID parameter. Open the file *"Views\models\index.cshtml"* and then add the following markup:

```
@model IEnumerable<FirstApp.Models.App>
@{
ViewBag.Title = "Index";
}
<h2>Index file</h2>
<p>
@Html.ActionLink("Create New", "Create")

@using (Html.BeginForm()){
<p> Title: @Html.TextBox("sString") <br />
<input type="submit" value="Filter" /></p>
}
</p>
```

Note that the code should be added immediately after the line "@Html.ActionLink("Create New", "Create")". The helper "Html.BeginForm" will create a <HTML> as the opening tag. If the user has clicked on the Filter button, this helper will cause this form to submit to itself. The Index method has no HttpPost overload. Since the method is just for filtering the data but not changing the state of the application, you don't need it.

The following HttpPost Index method would have been added. In such a situation, the action invoker will have matched the HttpPost Index method. Here is the method:

[HttpPost]

public string Index(FormCollection fc, string sString)

{

**   return "<h3> From [HttpPost]Index: " + sString + "</h3>";**

}

However, even after the addition of the "HttpPost" version of the Index method, a limitation exists in the way the implementation of this has been done. Suppose you need to bookmark a particular search and then send the link to your friends who will click and then view the list of all the filtered apps. You may have noticed we are using the same URL for both the HTTP POST and the HTTP GET requests and this URL is "localhost:xxxxx/Apps/Index".

To solve this problem, we just have to use an overload of the "BeginForm" and make it specify that our POST request should add search information to the URL and to route it to the HttpGet version of Index method. The existing BeginForm method, which has no parameters, should be replaced with the following:

@using

(Html.BeginForm("Index","Apps",FormMethod.Get))

Now after a search is posted, the URL will have a search query string. This searching will also be directed to the HttpGet Index, which is an action method, and this will have an HttpPost method.

Chapter 15- Creating a new Field

We want to make use of the code first migration availed by Entity Framework to move some of the changes to model classes and this change will affect the database.

Whenever a database is created automatically for you as we did earlier, a table is added to this database. This helps in syncing the schema of the database and the model classes. If the two are found not to be in sync, then the result will be an error. This is good for debugging purposes as errors will be detected and rectified early enough during the development process rather than during runtime.

How to set up Code First Migrations for Model Changes

Begin by opening the "*Solutions Explorer*". Right the file "*Apps.mdf*" and select "*Delete*".

This will delete the apps database from the machine. In case you fail to find this file, find the icon written *"Show All Files"* and then click on it. The icon is shown in the figure below:

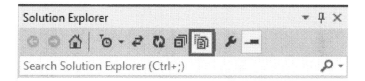

The figure below shows how to delete the apps database:

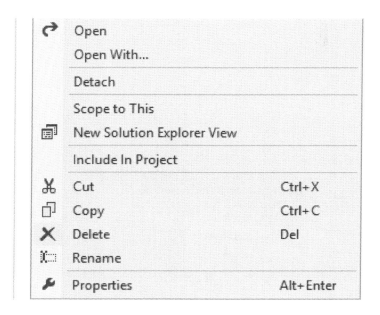

The next step is to build the application. This will ensure that it has no errors. Click on the *"Tools"* menu, choose *"Library Package Manager"* and then select *"Package Manager Console"*.

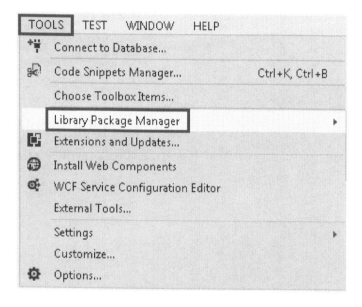

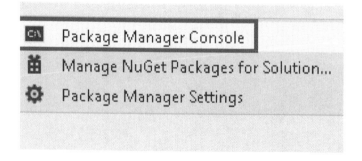

The console will appear with "*PM>*" prompt. Just press the "*Enter*" key and observe what will happen.

```
Checking if the context targets an existing database...
```

The command is called "*Enable-Migrations*" and it will create a file named "*Configurations.cs*" This will be done in the "*Migrations*" folder.

```
▷   ▓ App_Start
▷   ▢ bin
▷   ▓ Content
▷   ▓ Controllers
▷   ▓ img
┌─────────────────────────────────────┐
│ ◢   ▢ Migrations                     │
│        + C# Configuration.cs         │
└─────────────────────────────────────┘
▷   ▓ Models
▷   ▢ obj
▷   ▓ Scripts
▷   ▓ Views
      ▢ ▨ favicon.ico
```

The file "*Configuration.cs*" will then be opened in visual studio.

The method "*seed*" in this file "Configuration.cs" should be replaced with the following code:

```
protected override void
Seed(FirstApp.Models.AppDBContext context)
{

context.Apps.AddOrUpdate( j => j.Title,

new App

{

Title = "Downloader",

DevelopmentDate = DateTime.Parse("2014-3-11"),

Area = "Downloading",

Price = 2

},

new App

{

Title = "Music",

DevelopmentDate = DateTime.Parse("2013-3-12"),

Area = "Entertainment",

Price = 3
```

```csharp
    },
    new App
    {
        Title = "Calculator",
        DevelopmentDate = DateTime.Parse("2014-2-23"),
        Area = "Maths",
        Price = 2
    },
    new App
    {
        Title = "Browser",
        DevelopmentDate = DateTime.Parse("2012-4-20"),
        Area = "Internet",
        Price = 4
    }
);
}
```

You will notice that there is a red line under the word *"App"*.

Right click on it and then choose *"Resolve"*. Select *"Suing MvcApp.Models"*.

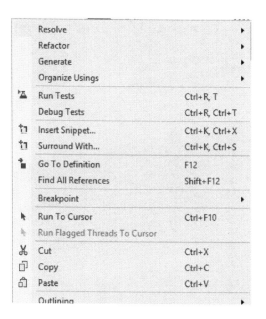

After doing the above, the following statement will be added at the top of the program:

using MvcApp.Models;

After every migration, Code First will call the method *"seed"*.
Rows which had been inserted will then the updated. In case
they do not exist, they will be inserted. To perform an *"Upsert"*
operation, we use the *"AddorUpdate"* operation as shown in the
following code:


```
context.Apps.AddOrUpdate(j => j.Title,

new App

{

Title = "Love",

DevelopmentDate = DateTime.Parse("2011-4-11"),

Area = "Romance",

Price = 1.5

}
```


Note that after every migration, the *"seed"* method will be run.
This means that we will not just insert the data, but much work
will be involved. In case you try to insert a row when the row
already exists, then the *"upsert"* method will show errors that
would result from this.

Any changes which you make will be overridden. Our aim is to perform a conditional insertion, in which we will insert the only rows which do not exist. We have specified the property that should be used in case a row is found. For this purpose, we have used the title of the app since it is unique for each application:

context.Apps.AddOrUpdate(j => j.Title,

Our code assumes that each app has a unique title. In case you insert a duplicate, then you will get the following exception:

SEQUENCE CONTAINS MORE THAN ONE ELEMENT

However, the above exception will be raised the next time you try to perform a migration.

Before doing any other step, build your project. This will prevent errors from occurring.

We want to create a *"DBMigration"* class for our initial migration.

Assuming that you have opened the *"Package Manage Console"* run the command *"add-migration Initial"*. This will create the initial migration.

A class file with the name *"{Datestamp}_Initial.cs"* will be created in the *"Migrations"* folder. This file will contain the code that is responsible for creation of a database schema. The file will also contain instructions which will guide you on how to create a table in the Apps database.

We now need to create the database. Open the *"Package Manager Console"* window and then run the command *"update-database"*. This is shown in the figure below:

This will create the database and then run the "method" seed. It is also possible that you will get an error, which will tell you that the table can't be created because it already exists. The cause of this is that you after deleting the database, you ran the application before running the *"update-database"* command on the terminal as shown in the above figure. To solve this, you have the delete the *"apps"*.

Run the command *"update-database"* once again. In case this doesn't solve the error, then you have to delete the whole of the migrations folder and then begin the whole process from the start. You can now run the application and observe the result that you will get. It should be as follows:

My First App

Index

create new

Title DevelopmentDate Area Price

Downloader 2014-3-11 Downloading 2

Music 2013-3-12 Entertainment 3

Calculator 2014-2-23 Maths 2

Browser 2012-4-20 Internet 4

The above figure shows that our data was successfully added to the database.

Adding a Rating property to App Model

We should start by adding a rating property to our *"App"* class which already exists. Open the file *"Models\App.cs"* and then add the following to it:

public string Rating { get; set; }

The complete code of the class *"App"* should be as follows:

```
public class App
{
public int id { get; set; }
public string Title { get; set; }


[Display(Name = "Development Date")]
[DataType(DataType.Date)]
[DisplayFormat(DataFormatString = "{0:yyyy-MM-dd}", ApplyFormatInEditMode = true)]
public DateTime DevelopmentDate { get; set; }
public string Area { get; set; }
public decimal Price { get; set; }
public string Rating { get; set; }
}
```

You can build your application by pressing *"Ctrl + Shift + B"*. Note that a new field has been added to the *"App"* class. We need to update the *"white list"* so as to include this field. This can be done as follows:

[Bind(Include = "id, Title, DevelopmentDate, Area, Price, Rating")]

So that the rating property can be displayed on the browser, you have to update the views. Open the file *"Index.cshtml"* in the *"\views\Apps"* directory. You then have to add the *"Rating"* column just after the price. The file should finally be as follows:

@model IEnumerable<MvcApp.Models.App>

@{

ViewBag.Title = "Index";

}

<h2>Index File</h2>

<p>

@Html.ActionLink("Create New", "Create")

```
@using        (Html.BeginForm("Index",        "Apps",
FormMethod.Get))
{

<p>

Genre: @Html.DropDownList("appArea", "All")

Title: @Html.TextBox("sString")

<input type="submit" value="Filter" />

</p>

}

</p>

<table class="table">

<tr>

<th>

@Html.DisplayNameFor(model => model.Title)

</th>

<th>

@Html.DisplayNameFor(model =>
model.DevelopmentDate)

</th>

<th>

@Html.DisplayNameFor(model => model.Area)
```

```
</th>

<th>

@Html.DisplayNameFor(model => model.Price)

</th>

<th>

@Html.DisplayNameFor(model => model.Rating)

</th>

<th></th>

</tr>

@foreach (var it in Model) {

<tr>

<td>

@Html.DisplayFor(modelItem => it.Title)

</td>

<td>

@Html.DisplayFor(modelItem =>
item.DevelopmentDate)

</td>

<td>

@Html.DisplayFor(modelItem => it.Area)
```

```
</td>

<td>

@Html.DisplayFor(modelItem => it.Price)

</td>

<td>

@Html.DisplayFor(modelItem => it.Rating)

</td>

<td>

@Html.ActionLink("Edit", "Edit", new { id=it.id }) |

@Html.ActionLink("Details", "Details", new { id=it.id
}) |

@Html.ActionLink("Delete", "Delete", new { id=it.id
})

</td>

</tr>

}

</table>
```

In each of the output, the following columns should be shown:

My First App

Index

create new

Title DevelopmentDate Area Price Rating

As shown in the above figure, the column *"Rating"* has been added to our file. When creating a new app, we use a form to specify our details. We need to add a text field for the *"Rating"* which will allow the users to specify the rating for their new app. This can be done by modifying the *"\Views\Apps\Create.cs"* file to the following:

```
<div class="form-group">

@Html.LabelFor(model => model.Price, new { @class
= "control-label col-md-2" })

<div class="col-md-10">

@Html.EditorFor(model => model.Price)

@Html.ValidationMessageFor(model =>
model.Price)

</div>
```

```
</div>

<div class="form-group">

@Html.LabelFor(model => model.Rating, new {
@class = "control-label col-md-2" })

<div class="col-md-10">

@Html.EditorFor(model => model.Rating)

@Html.ValidationMessageFor(model =>
model.Rating)

</div>

</div>

<div class="form-group">

<div class="col-md-offset-2 col-md-10">

<input type="submit" value="Create" class="btn btn-
default" />

</div>

</div>

</div>

}


<div>

@Html.ActionLink("View the List", "Index")
```

```
</div>

@section Scripts {

@Scripts.Render("~/bundles/jqueryval")

}
```

After the above modification, the new form for creating a new app should be as follows:

Title: [   ]

DevelopmentDate: [   ]

Area: [   ]

Price: [   ]

Rating: [   ]

[Submit]

The figure shows that there is a text field where the user can specify the rating of the app while creating or entering its details into the database.

The "*seed*" method also needs to be updated so that there is a value for the newly created column, that is, the "*Rating*" column. It should be as follows:

new App

{

Title = "Downloader",

DevelopmentDate = DateTime.Parse("2014-3-11"),

Area = "Downloading",

Rating= "PF"

Price = 2

},

},

You can build the application.

Chapter 16- Validating the Fields

We want to be able to validate the details which we provide to the "*Apps*" model. This validation should be applied whenever the user is creating a new application or while changing the details of an already existing application.

This should be done in such a way that repetitions will be avoided by all means possible. This means that we should implement the functionality in one class which should be applied to all other classes. This will ensure that there is minimal coding thus saving on time. Let us add validation to the "*App*" model. Open the "*App.cs*" class and replace the existing code with the following:

```
public class App
{
public int id { get; set; }
[StringLength(50, MinimumLength = 4)]
public string Title { get; set; }
```

```
[Display(Name = "Development Date")]

[DataType(DataType.Date)]

[DisplayFormat(DataFormatString = "{0:yyyy-MM-
dd}", ApplyFormatInEditMode = true)]

public DateTime DevelopmentDate { get; set; }

[RegularExpression(@"^[A-Z]+[a-zA-Z"-'\s]*$")]

[Required]

[StringLength(35)]

public string Genre { get; set; }

[Range(1, 99)]

[DataType(DataType.Currency)]

public decimal Price { get; set; }

[RegularExpression(@"^[A-Z]+[a-zA-Z"-'\s]*$")]

[StringLength(6)]

public string Rating { get; set; }

}
```

The maximum length for the title has been set to 50 characters

and it can only take a minimum of 4 characters. Note that for

the string types, only special characters that you have specified

will be accepted; otherwise, you will get errors.

We have set the maximum of our strings using the method "*StringLength*". This limitation is also applied to our database. This means that our database schema will also change. Click on "*Server Explorer*" to open it. Right click the "*Apps*" table and then choose "*Open Table Definition*". Observe the datatypes of our table columns which should be as follows:

Data Type	Allow Nulls	Default	
int	☐		
nvarchar(MAX)	☑		
datetime	☐		
nvarchar(MAX)	☑		
decimal(18,2)	☐		
nvarchar(MAX)	☑		
	☐		

As shown in the above figure, the columns have been set to the "*MAX*" property. We now need to update the database schema. Open the "*Package Manager Console*" window and then run the following commands:

add-migration DataAnnotations

update-database

The following code will update the constraints of the schema:

```
public override void Update()
{
AlterColumn("dbo.Apps", "Title", c =>
c.String(maxLength: 50));

AlterColumn("dbo.Apps", "Area", c =>
c.String(nullable: false, maxLength: 30));

AlterColumn("dbo.Apps", "Rating", c =>
c.String(maxLength: 5));

}
```

With the above codes, the *"Area"* field cannot be left empty, meaning that it must be specified for each of the applications that the user tries to create. You can also see the values which we have specified the number of characters to in each of the fields. Consider the code given below:

```
AppDBContext db = new AppDBContext();

App app = new App();

app.Title = "This is my application";

db.Apps.Add(app);

db.SaveChanges();      // <= an validation exception
will be thrown on the server side
```

We have created an instance of the AppDBConext and this has been given the name "db". An instance of the App has also been created and then named "app". This process is known as 'instantiation'. The above program will throw the following exception when run:

Validation   failed   is   for   one   or   more   entities. See"'EntityValidationErrors' property for more details. This is shown in the figure below:

Validation failed for one or more entities. See 'EntityValidationErrors' property for more details.

Note that before the changes we made to the model are saved to the database, the rules of validation must first be saved by calling the "*saveChanges*" method. This explains the source of the above exception. It is good to make use of the validation rules imposed by .NET automatically. This will ensure that every field has been validated and that no bad data will be allowed into the database. You can now run the application. Navigate to the form for creating a new application. It should be as follows:

Title:

DevelopmentDate:

Area:

Price:

Rating:

Submit

Try to enter data which does not conform what we have validated. You will get errors. In my case, I have not specified the field *"Title"* but we had declared that it should not be null. I get the following error:

The Title field is required.

The above figure shows that our validation worked correctly.

Conclusion

It can be concluded that ASP.NET MVC 5 is a framework used for web development. The framework is open-source, meaning that you can download and use it for free. It has three parts, namely the Model, the View and the Controller. The controller represents where the real logic is done as the entire processing takes place in this layer. This shows how important this layer is.

The view is responsible for handling rendering of the output. This means that it is the user interface which users are able to interact with by either reading the output they get after processing has been done or providing data to the system for processing. The model represents where the data is stored, meaning that it is the database for the application. The controller is at the center of the two other layers. It is possible for the view to communicate directly with the model.

However, this is not encouraged as your application will not be easy to maintain, test and debug in case errors occur.

Web developers are encouraged to make use of the controller whereby the view must communicate to it so that it can relay data to the model. The same case applies to the model, in which it must communicate with the controller first to reach the view. Note that there are view templates which you can make use of to enhance the look of the user interface for rendering output to the user. ASP.NET MVC 5 can make use of the database. If you create a form where the user can provide the data for input, make sure that you validate the form. This will ensure that no bad data is entered into the database.

In case your code makes use of a database which you have not created, then it will be automatically created for you. It is also possible to retrieve data stored in the database with ASP.NET MVC 5 for viewing by the users. There is a need to know how to use visual studio to add a model, view and controller to your web app.

Made in the USA
Columbia, SC
15 May 2017